Adler, Ann
German family—(Beans)
1. Family—Germany—Munich—Juvenile Literature
I. Title
306.9′5′094336 HQ626.5.M/
ISBN 0-7136-2390-X

A & C Black (Publishers) Limited
35 Bedford Row, London WC1R4JH

Acknowledgments
The map is by Tony Garrett

ISBN 0-7136-2390-X

Filmset by August Filmsetting, Warrington, Cheshire
Colour origination by Hongkong Graphic Arts Service Centre, Hong Kong
Printed in Great Britain by Hazell Watson and Viney Ltd. Aylesbury, Bucks

German Family

Ann Adler

Photographs by Chris Fairclough

Adam & Charles Black · London

My name is Renate Blattner, but everyone calls me Reni. I'm eleven years old and I live in a town called Mainburg. It's a small town, about 10 000 people live there. Mainburg is only 60 kilometres from Munich. That's the third largest city in West Germany and the capital of Bavaria. Bavaria is one of the Federal States of West Germany.

My parents' names are Hans and Helga. And there's my brother Christian, too. He is two years older than I am.

We live in the same house as my mum's parents. They have the flat upstairs and we live downstairs. We have two bedrooms, a living room, a kitchen and a bathroom in our flat. It's a bit small for the four of us, but that doesn't matter, as we won't be living here much longer. Soon we're going to have a whole house to ourselves. I'll have my own room and won't have to share one with Christian any more. I'm looking forward to that!

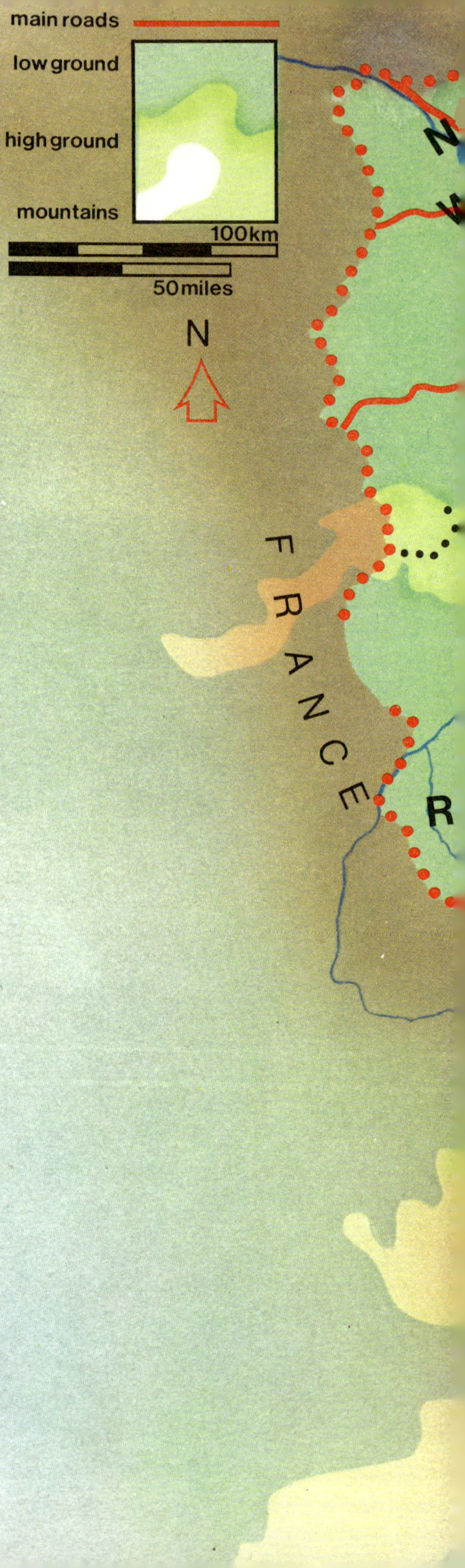

HRHINE
TPHALIA
Dortmund
sseldorf
ologne
onn
HESS
Frankfurt
ELLE
ELAND
PFALZ
R RHINE
BAVARIA
Nuremberg
CZECHOSLOVAKIA
Stuttgart
BARDEN
WURTTEMBERG
Ulm
R
DANUBE
Wolnzach
Mainburg
Sandelshausen
Munich
Salzburg
Basel
Zurich
SWITZERLAND
The Alps
AUSTRIA
NORWAY
SWEDEN
GREAT
BRITAIN
EIRE
NORTH SEA
DENMARK
BALTIC
SEA
London
HOLLAND
Berlin
POLAND
WEST
GERMANY
EAST
Paris
CZECHO-
SLOVAKIA
ATLANTIC
OCEAN
FRANCE
Munich
AUSTRIA
SWITZ
ITALY
YUGOSLAVIA
SPAIN
MEDITERRANEAN

Dad is building our new house himself. He works on the building site on Saturdays, and every afternoon when he comes home from work until it gets dark. Mum gets a bit fed up sometimes, she says dad is always working and needs to relax. But it will be worth it when the house is ready. Mum says we all have to help so that the house is finished quickly.

Today, my grandfather and my uncle have come to help lay the bricks for the first floor of the house. We're standing in the living room! I'm allowed to spread the mortar, but dad and grandad put the bricks in place. Dad says it will be at least six months before we can move in.

Our new house is in Sandelshausen, the village next to Mainburg. But I will still be going to the same school in Mainburg. I'll just have to get up a bit earlier to catch the school bus. Now, the bus picks us up at a quarter to eight in the morning. About six of us catch the bus at the same place, but I always sit next to my friend Brigitte. She's the girl in the pink jacket.

School starts at eight o'clock and finishes at one o'clock. There aren't any lessons in the afternoon, but we can stay on to do sports or music if we want. On Mondays, I stay on at school for a dance and keep-fit class. We do lots of different exercises and the teacher always plays good music. She knows all the latest dances, too. I always learn the new dances so I'll know how to do them when I go to parties.

It's my first year at this school. The school is called a Hauptschule. The building is very modern and much bigger than my old school was. There are 800 pupils. All the classrooms are grouped around a big hall. On rainy days, we sit in the hall at break-time.

Christian's school is called a Gymnasium. His school is right next to mine, but I never see him during school time. He leaves home earlier than I do and takes a different bus to and from school.

I'm in form 6C and my form teacher is Mrs Greilinger. She teaches us German, Maths, Physics and Geography. Geography is my favourite subject and I've got a special set of coloured pencils just for drawing maps. I also learn English, History and Biology.

We have five or six lessons every morning. There is a five minute break between lessons, and a long break at half-past nine. If it isn't raining, we all go out into the school yard for the long break. I bring a sandwich and a carton of milk with me, or I buy something to eat at the school kiosk. Here I am with my friend Brigitte. Usually, I try to avoid her at break-time because she always wants to swap sandwiches with me.

Dad leaves for work very early in the morning, when we are still asleep. He works in Munich and he has to be at work by seven o'clock. Many people from Mainburg work in Munich. There isn't much industry in Mainburg, so there aren't enough jobs for all the people who live here.

Dad works for a company called BMW. They make motor cars. You have probably seen BMW cars in the street. This one is ours. Dad says they are the best cars in the world. One of dad's friends works for Volkswagen, another German car company, and they are always arguing about which cars are the best. Dad doesn't use his car to go to work, though. There is a company bus which picks him up in the morning and brings him home in the afternoon.

BMW produce about 900 cars each day. The cars are sold in Germany and other countries all over the world. There are 25 000 people working for the company. Not all of them work in the car factory, of course. Some of them work in offices.

The offices are in a very tall building. Once, dad took me right up to the top of the offices. When you look down, you can see how enormous the BMW factory is. From the other side of the offices, you can see the Olympic Stadium of Munich. This is where the Olympic Games were held in 1972. Now, anyone can go there and use the swimming pools and the tennis courts. There are big football matches in the stadium. When *TSV München 1860* play there, my father and Christian always go to watch. *TSV München 1860* is the football team which they support.

My dad knows all about cars. He used to work on the production line – that's where the cars are built. Now he teaches the apprentices who are doing their training at the factory. There are more than 600 apprentices at BMW. Most of them are boys, but there are some girls, too. They have a huge workshop for their lessons. Dad says it's very noisy with all the banging and drilling.

In the first year, my dad teaches the apprentices metalwork. He shows them how to cut and shape metal and how to drill holes in it. The apprentices have to know all about the different tools that are used for working with metal. Later on, they learn all about car engines.

The apprentices have to understand how an engine works, and they have to be able to take one apart and put it all back together again. They also learn how the different parts of a car are put together on the production line – how the bonnet is fitted, how a door is built, how the seats are installed and many other things.

At the end of the third year, the apprentices have to take an exam. So dad must make sure they understand everything he teaches them. If his students pass the exam, they are qualified to work as car mechanics, fitters, welders or metalworkers. They either stay on and get a job with BMW, or they go and work somewhere else. This is Thomas, he was one of dad's best students. Now he works as a fitter. Here he's helping to test the engine of a new car on the production line.

Dad gets home from work at four o'clock. He only has sandwiches for lunch, so mum cooks a hot meal for him in the evening. The rest of us have our main meal at lunchtime. Mum has it ready for us when we get home from school. She doesn't go to work, so she spends the morning going shopping, doing the housework and the cooking. Mum does a lot of gardening, too. She's very proud of our garden, we have lovely flowers in the front garden and vegetables in the back garden.

After lunch, Christian and I take turns to help with the washing-up. Then we have to do our homework. Mum lets us work in the living room because our room is too small. We get homework to do every day. But sometimes we just don't feel like getting down to it, so we have a game of cards first. It's no good trying to persuade mum to play, though. She always says she has too much work to do.

Christian loves to do woodwork. He builds all sorts of things. He has made a model aeroplane and some loudspeaker boxes, and he's always working on something new. He has a workbench in the basement. As soon as Christian has finished his homework, he disappears down there.

I like to go cycling, and I always use my bicycle to go and see my friends. We meet by the fountain in the main square, have a chat and watch people go by.

Sometimes, we ride out to the countryside and visit my friend Susanne's grandad. He's a farmer, so he is always working, even on Saturdays. Here we are trying to persuade him to give us a ride on his tractor.

Susanne's grandad keeps cows and pigs on his farm, and he grows hops. You can see the hops in this picture. They are held up by tall poles. As the plants grow, they wind up these poles. When the hops are ripe, Susanne's grandad picks and dries them. The hops are used for brewing beer. There are hop fields all around Mainburg. It is one of the biggest hop growing areas in Europe.

If Susanne's grandad is too busy to see us, we go for a walk in the forest. Very tall pine trees grow there. Some parts of the forest are dark and spooky, so its a good place for playing games of hide and seek. We call it Verstecken.

In the evening, I often stay home and watch television. There are three German television channels, but we can also watch the Austrian programmes. That's because the border between Germany and Austria isn't far from here. Once a week, there's a television programme with all the new pop songs which I like to watch. Christian likes to watch sports programmes. Tonight there is an important football match on, so we have to watch that.

On Saturdays, I help mum with the shopping. We have to do it all in the morning because the shops close at lunchtime. During the week, the shops stay open until six or half-past six.

Today, we're a bit late, so the bakery has almost sold out. The bakery is called Bäckerei Müller. You can buy all kinds of bread there – long loaves of wholemeal bread, round loaves made of sour-dough and a very dark kind of bread called Pumpernickel which you buy already sliced in a packet. They also have plain white bread and small rolls. I buy a large loaf of white bread and a Bretzel. You can see a whole plate of Bretzels on top of the counter. They are crunchy and have salt on the outside, so they make you very thirsty.

Next, we go to the butcher. The shop is called Metzgerei Schäfle. It's right next to a restaurant. The butcher sells a large selection of sausages and cold meats, as well as ordinary meat like chops and roasts. The sausages usually have to be cooked, but some can be eaten cold. There is Weißwurst, a long white sausage, Servelat and frankfurters, which we call Würstchen. The cold meat is called Aufschnitt. The butcher slices it for you. My mum often buys smoked or cooked ham.

Saturday is the day when I get my pocket money. I get three Marks a week. Sometimes mum lets me go to a cafe with my friends after we have finished the shopping. Going to a cafe is a special treat for me. I save up enough money to buy a piece of cake and a fizzy drink or a big ice-cream with lots of whipped cream on top. Even the smallest cafe in Mainburg has at least ten different kinds of cake to choose from. A piece of cake costs about two Marks, and a fizzy drink one Mark and fifty Pfennig.

Sunday is the only day of the week when we all have breakfast together. We have bread with slices of cold sausage, or jam, and we drink coffee with milk. Once in a while, we even have a piece of cake.

After Sunday breakfast, Christian and I go to church. At Christmas and Easter, and on other important holidays, my parents come too. But usually they like to stay at home and relax. Mum says it is the only time when she and dad can have a quiet time together.

Our family is Catholic, like most people in Bavaria. There are three churches in Mainburg. The service we go to is held in the biggest one. It's on the main square.

For going to church, and on other special occasions, I often wear my Dirndl. That's a traditional Bavarian dress. My Dirndl is made of blue material with a fine pattern. The sleeves are white lace, and I wear a red apron with the dress. I never wear my Dirndl to school. I wear a skirt or a pair of trousers. We don't have a school uniform.

Sunday lunch is always a big meal. Often, my grandparents come downstairs and we all eat together. Today we are having soup to begin with. Then we are having meat with gravy, potatoes, vegetables, Knödl and a salad. Knödl are a special kind of dumpling made of bread. They taste nice with the gravy. For dessert, there is a fruit trifle. I try not to eat too much of the first courses, so I'll have plenty of room left for trifle.

My father was born in Czechoslovakia. He came to Mainburg with his mother when he was a very young boy. Dad's mother died a few years ago. Every weekend, dad drives to Wolnzach, a nearby village, and puts fresh flowers on his mother's grave. Christian and I go with him. We light a candle on the grave and make sure the flowers are arranged nicely.

My mother was born in Mainburg and has never lived anywhere else. Many of her relatives live in and around Mainburg. We often see my uncle and aunt. They drop in on Sunday afternoon, or we go to visit them. They have a little baby girl. If my aunt is busy, she leaves the baby with my grandmother. Then I always go upstairs to my grandmother's flat to play with the baby and help look after her. I love doing that.

Every autumn, there is a famous fair in Munich. It's called Oktoberfest. Thousands of people from all over the world come to Munich, just for the fair. It goes on for two weeks. I spend a day there with Christian and my parents every year.

We drive to Munich on the Autobahn. That's a motorway with two or three lanes. Dad likes driving on the Autobahn because you are allowed to go very fast, up to 130 kilometres an hour.

There is an awful lot of traffic in the city and it's hard to find a place to park. We leave the car on the outskirts of Munich and take an underground train to the centre. The underground was only built a few years ago. There used to be only trams and buses in Munich. You can see a tram in the picture. They drive along the streets on tracks and are attached to wires overhead.

The underground stations are very modern. There aren't any ticket offices. You have to buy your ticket from a machine. We never know which buttons to press and we have to look at a special map to work out what type of ticket to get. Even people who live in the city often have to do this!

At the Oktoberfest, the fairground is enormous. I stick close to mum and dad, in case I get lost. There are roller-coasters, bumper-cars, swings, ghost-trains and all sorts of other rides. I don't like the roller-coasters and the ghost-trains much, but Christian and I go on some of the smaller rides. They are quite expensive, so dad doesn't allow us to go too often. We don't want to spend all our pocket money yet because there are lots of other things to do.

There are big tents where people sit at long tables and drink beer. We stop at lots of different stalls which sell grilled sausages, sandwiches with pickled herrings, ice-cream, candy floss, sugared almonds and cold drinks. Christian and I try as many different things as we can. By the end of the day, Christian has spent all his pocket money but I still have a bit left. I buy myself a Lebkuchenherz. It's a honey cake, shaped like a heart. The cake is decorated with sugar and usually has a funny saying on it.

I'm much too full to eat my honey cake, so I hang it round my neck. In fact, after so many different kinds of food and all the rides, I'm beginning to feel a bit sick. So I'm pleased when mum says it's time to go home to Mainburg.